Love to Dress Up
18" Doll Clothes

I have to pinch myself some days to wake up to the fact that I am living a dream. I get to create new things every day, and to top it off, my latest endeavor involves dressing dolls. My best friend, other than my little sister, when I was growing up was my doll, Margaret. The fact that Margaret was a "city girl" kind of doll, which was far different from my simple farm life, provided my imagination with unending scenarios that Margaret and I experienced hand in hand.

You guessed it already, I am sure—I was one of those girls who made doll clothes before I could sew. I managed to fashion the latest in trendy outfits from discarded socks and old shirts, referencing the latest Sears catalog for my fashion advice, adding simple drawings to the discarded clothing items to imitate the colors and patterns from the pages of the catalog. Unfortunately, due to a number of moves with my family, I do not have access to any of those first designs, but I am sure they would provide a host of warm memories and most likely a few good laughs.

I chose to design the outfits in this book using fat quarters for a number of reasons. First and foremost, is their size, which is absolutely perfect for creating doll clothes. The second reason is all of the wonderful displays of fat quarters in fabric stores these days—carefully crafted display after display, filled to the brim with tightly wrapped bundles of precut fabric coordinated by style, color or pattern. Choosing your favorites might take some time, but honestly, what better way is there to spend a few minutes? My final reason for choosing fat quarters is the ease with which you can purchase a fat quarter; simply choose your favorite and head to the cash register.

I hope you have as much fun making the outfits within the pages of this book as I did designing them for you. Have fun choosing the fabric, sewing the outfits and helping create childhood memories for that someone special in your life.

Sew far Sew good,

Lorine

Meet the Designer

Lorine Mason is an author, project designer and regular columnist whose work has been featured in print, on the Web and television. She works with a variety of art mediums, combining them with her enthusiasm for all things fabric. She strives to create items others will be inspired to re-create, hopefully adding their own personal touches. Her creative career started in retail, weaving its way through management and education positions along the path. This experience, along with a goal to stay on top of trends in color and style, gives her current work the edge manufacturers, publishers and editors have come to expect. She shares her life with husband, Bill, and daughters, Jocelyn and Kimbrely. They currently live in Virginia having moved there from Winnipeg, Manitoba, by way of Beaconsfield, Quebec.

House of White Birches, Berne, Indiana 46711   DRGnetwork.com

General Instructions

Project Note

Measurements for 18-inch girl dolls vary from manufacturers; pattern adjustment to accommodate those variations may be needed.

Fabric Selection

All of the outfits and accessories in this book were made using fat quarters. Available in colorful patterns and packaging, fat quarters are the "candy" in the fabric store and are a wonderful way to coordinate fabrics. Generally available in 18 x 22-inch cuts, fat quarters are equivalent to standard 9 x 45-inch quarter yards, and any cotton fabric is suitable for these patterns.

Basic Sewing Supplies & Equipment

- Sewing machine and matching thread
- Scissors of various sizes, including pinking shears
- Rotary cutter(s), mats and straightedges
- Pattern-tracing paper or cloth
- Pressing tools such as sleeve rolls and June Tailor boards
- Pressing equipment, including ironing board and iron; press cloths
- Straight pins and pincushion
- Measuring tools
- Marking pens (either air- or water-soluble) or tailor's chalk
- Seam sealant
- Hand-sewing needles and thimble
- Point turners

Optional Supplies:
- ¼-inch-wide double-sided basting tape
- Tube-turning tool
- Mini iron
- Serger

Construction & Application Techniques

General Construction

Fill multiple bobbins ahead of time with neutral colors of thread. A cream-colored thread was used for many of the garments in this book. Change only the top color of thread to either match or contrast with garment colors.

Backstitch at the beginning and end of each seam to secure stitching.

For longer wear and cleaner construction, finish raw edges using preferred method.

Gathering

1. Make two rows of longer-than-normal stitches on either side of the seam line, leaving long thread tails at either end (Figure 1).

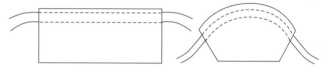

Figure 1

2. With right sides together, pin gathered section to appropriate garment section at each end and at the center (Figure 2).

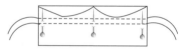

Figure 2

3. Pull bobbin threads at one end to gather. When half of gathered section fits straight-edge length, secure bobbin threads by twisting around pin (Figure 3). Repeat for second half of section. Pin securely along seam line, adjusting gathers evenly.

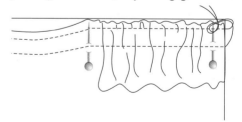

Figure 3

4. Stitch at seam line with gathered section on top (Figure 4). Keep gathers even so folds of fabric do not form while stitching.

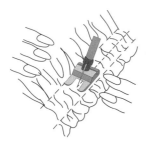

Figure 4

5. Remove gathering stitches after sewing seam.

Bias-Tape Application

Bound Edges

1. Leaving bias tape folded, sandwich raw edges of garment between bias tape so the fabric raw edge meets the center fold of the bias tape (Figure 5).

Figure 5

2. Edgestitch bias tape to secure (Figure 6). *Note: Purchased bias tape has one side wider than the other. Be sure to edgestitch with shorter side up when using purchased bias tape.*

Figure 6

Bias-Tape Hems & Casings

1. Press center fold of bias tape flat, leaving edges folded (Figure 7).

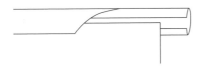

Figure 7

2. Pin raw edge of bias tape along fabric raw edge and stitch in edge fold (Figure 8).

Figure 8

3. Press bias tape to wrong side and stitch along edge fold (Figure 9).

Figure 9

Collars

1. Mark collar neckline center. Pin and stitch collar sections right sides together using a ¼-inch seam allowance. Do not stitch neckline seam (Figure 10).

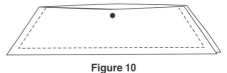

Figure 10

2. Carefully clip curves on rounded collars, and trim points on pointed collars (Figure 11). Turn, using point turner in corners. Press.

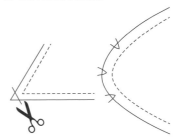

Figure 11

3. Pin, and then baste collar to garment neckline, matching collar center to garment center back (Figure 12).

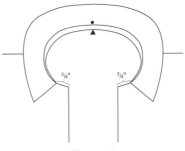

Figure 12

4. Collar will be stitched in place when facing is applied.

House of White Birches, Berne, Indiana 46711   DRGnetwork.com

Facings

1. Stitch facings together at center back seam (Figure 13). Press seam open.

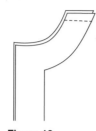

Figure 13

2. Apply bias tape to outside edges (Figure 14). **Note:** *Refer to general instructions on bias-tape application for bound edges.*

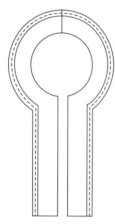

Figure 14

3. Pin facing to garment neckline and front edges, right sides together. Stitch using ¼-inch seam allowance (Figure 15).

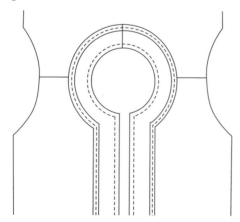

Figure 15

4. Clip curves and trim corners (Figure 16). Turn to right side and press.

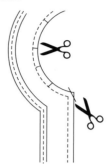

Figure 16

5. Edgestitch facing through all layers using coordinating thread (Figure 17).

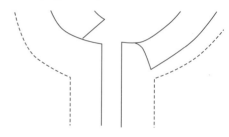

Figure 17

Sleeves

1. Stitch two rows of gathering stitches at sleeve cap (Figure 18). **Note:** *Refer to general instructions on gathering (page 2).*

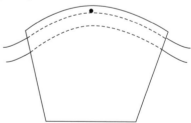

Figure 18

2. With right sides together, pin sleeve cap center to garment shoulder seam and edges of sleeve to garment sides (Figure 19). Gather sleeve cap to fit garment armhole and pin securely.

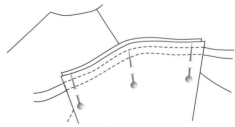

Figure 19

3. Stitch using a ¼-inch seam allowance. Press seam allowance toward sleeve (Figure 20).

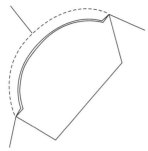

Figure 20

4. With right sides together, match armhole seams and pin underarm seam. Stitch using a ¼-inch seam allowance (Figure 21).

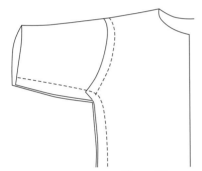

Figure 21

Hems

Single hem

1. Press at least ¼ inch to wrong side of garment (Figure 22).

Figure 22

2. Measuring from the folded edge just made, press the hem width indicated in individual instructions to garment wrong side. (Figure 23).

Figure 23

3. Edgestitch close to second fold (Figure 24).

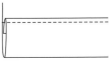

Figure 24

4. If desired, use a contrasting thread to add a simple decorative finish to hems.

Double-turned ¼-inch hem

1. Press ¼ inch to wrong side of section (Figure 25).

Figure 25

2. Turn and press again ¼ inch to wrong side. Edgestitch close to second fold (Figure 26).

Figure 26

Fastener Application

1. Try finished garment on doll to determine where fasteners should be positioned to fit doll's girth.

2. Mark position with pin, lapping garment right side over left (Figure 27).

Figure 27

3. Sew male side of snap to right side and female side of snap to left side of garment (Figure 28).

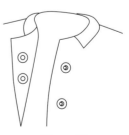

Figure 28

Topstitching

Machine-stitch approximately ⅛ inch on each side of the seam line. *Note: Because of the narrow seam allowances used in these patterns, it is recommended that topstitching be done from the wrong side.* ❖

Shirttails & Casual Pants

Materials
- Coordinating fat quarters:
    - 1 print
    - 1 stripe
- 1 package ¼-inch coordinating bias tape
- Four ½-inch buttons
- 11 inches ¼-inch-wide elastic
- 2 size-1/0 snap fasteners
- Basic sewing supplies and equipment

Cutting
Use pattern templates A through G, following cutting lines for Shirttails.
Transfer pattern markings to fabric pieces.

From print fat quarter:
- Cut one shirt back (C) on fold.
- Cut two shirt fronts (D), reversing one.
- Cut two sleeves (E).
- Cut two collars (F) on fold.
- Cut two facings (G), reversing one.
- Cut one 2½ x 2½-inch square for shirt pocket.
- Cut two 1¼ x 9-inch strips for pants-leg hem bands.

From stripe fat quarter:
Cut pieces for pants fronts and backs with stripes running vertically.
- Cut two pants backs (A), reversing one.
- Cut two pants fronts (B), reversing one.
- Cut two 2½ x 3-inch pieces for pants pockets.

Assembly
Stitch right sides together using a ¼-inch seam allowance unless otherwise specified. Refer to General Instructions (page 2) throughout for specific construction techniques.

Shirttails
1. Sew shirt fronts and back together at shoulder seams. Press seams open.

2. Construct and stitch collar to shirt neckline (see page 3).

3. Construct and stitch facings to shirt (see page 4).

4. Stitch a double-turned ¼-inch hem in bottom edge of each sleeve.

5. Construct and stitch sleeves to garment (see page 4).

6. Press under ½ inch along top edge of pocket and ¼ inch along sides and bottom edges. Center and stitch button to pocket top.

7. Pin pocket to left-hand side of shirt front 1 inch from front edge and 3 inches from shoulder seam (Figure 1). Topstitch along sides and bottom of pocket.

Figure 1

8. Open and press bias-tape center fold flat. Turning under ¼ inch at each end, pin bias tape to bottom edge of shirt, right sides together. Stitch on fold line of bias tape (Figure 2a). Press bias tape to inside of shirt. Topstitch along top folded edge and short ends of bias tape (Figure 2b).

Figure 2a   **Figure 2b**

9. Sew snaps to front opening, lapping right front over left front. Sew three buttons to shirt right front, placing first button two inches from top and spacing lower buttons 1¼ inches (Figure 3).

Figure 3

Casual Pants
1. Stitch one pants fronts to one pants backs along side seams. Repeat for remaining front and back pieces. Press seams open.

2. On each pants pocket, press under ½ inch along top edge and ¼ inch along sides and bottom edges.

Love to Dress Up 18" Doll Clothes

3. Center and pin pockets over side seams at positions marked on templates. Topstitch along sides and bottom edges of each pocket.

4. Stitch pants center front (Figure 4). Press seam open.

Figure 4

5. Using a serger or a zigzag stitch, finish top raw edge of pants. Press to wrong side along casing fold line. Stitch ⅜ inch from folded edge to create casing for elastic.

6. Thread elastic through casing. Pin ends of elastic even with back seam of pants and stitch to secure (Figure 5).

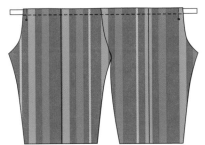

Figure 5

7. On one long edge of each pants-leg hem band, press under ¼ inch. Stitch long raw edges to bottoms of pant legs. Trim band to pant-leg width (Figure 6).

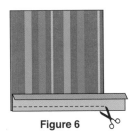   

Figure 6   **Figure 7**

8. On each pants leg, fold hem band over seam allowance to wrong side. Press and topstitch strip (Figure 7).

9. Stitch pants center back seam. Press seam open. Sew inner leg seams to complete pants. ❖

House of White Birches, Berne, Indiana 46711   DRGnetwork.com

Striped Tank & Walking Shorts

Materials
- 2 matching striped fat quarters
- 8 (½-inch) buttons
- 11 inches ¼-inch-wide elastic
- 2 size-1/0 snap fasteners
- Basic sewing supplies and equipment

Cutting
Use pattern templates H, I, J, K and L.
Transfer pattern markings to fabric pieces.

From striped fat quarters:
With stripes running vertically:
- Cut two top bodice backs (H), reversing one.
- Cut one top bodice front (I) on fold.
- Cut one lower front/back (K) on fold.
- Cut two shorts (L), reversing one.
- Cut one 1¾ x 2¼-inch piece for shorts pocket.

With stripes running horizontally:
- Cut two back contrast waistbands (J), reversing one.
- Cut one 6¼ x 1½-inch strip for front contrast waistband.

On the bias:
- Cut and piece ¾ x 44-inch strip for bias binding. *Note: See Making Bias Tape on page 10.*

Assembly
Stitch right sides together using ¼-inch seam allowance unless otherwise specified. Refer to General Instructions (page 2) throughout for specific construction techniques.

Striped Tank
1. Stitch tank bodice front and backs together at shoulder seams. Press seams open.

2. Referring to Making Bias Tape on page 10, use bias-binding strip to make ¼-inch bias tape. Apply bias tape to neckline and armhole edges.

3. Stitch front contrast waistband to bottom of bodice front. Repeat, stitching back contrast waistbands to bottoms of bodice back sections (Figure 1). Press seams toward waistbands.

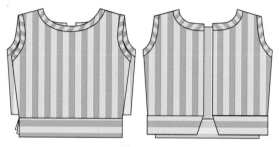

Figure 1

4. Stitch bodice side seams. Press seams open.

5. Stitch lower front/back to bottom edge of waistband (Figure 2). Press seam toward waistband.

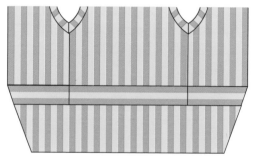

Figure 2

6. Stitch double-turned ¼-inch hem along tank back and bottom edges.

7. Sew snaps to tank back opening, lapping left over right. Center and sew three buttons to front waistband. Center and sew three buttons down center back of tank (Figure 3).

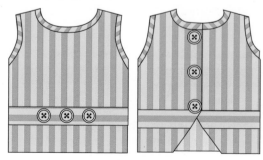

Figure 3

Walking Shorts

1. Apply bias tape to top edge of pocket. Press under ¼ inch along sides and bottom of pocket.

2. Center pocket on shorts left leg where indicated. Topstitch along sides and bottom of pocket (Figure 4).

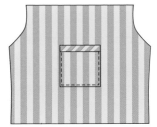

Figure 4

3. Stitch center front seam of shorts.

4. Using a serger or zigzag stitch, finish top raw edge of shorts. Turn finished edge to wrong side along casing fold line; press. Stitch ⅜ inch from folded edge to create elastic casing (Figure 5).

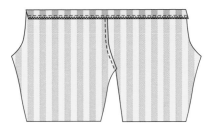

Figure 5

5. Thread elastic through casing. Pin elastic ends even with center back seam of shorts and stitch to secure.

6. Apply bias tape to shorts-leg bottoms.

7. Stitch center back seam. Press seam open.

8. Sew inner leg seams.

9. Center and sew a button to side of each pant leg slightly above bias binding (Figure 6). ❖

Figure 6

House of White Birches, Berne, Indiana 46711   DRGnetwork.com

Making Bias Tape

Make your own bias tape to add a distinctive flair to any project. Instructions are for ¼-inch finished-size bias tape.

1. Fold fabric diagonally so crosswise grain straight edge is parallel to selvage or lengthwise grain. Cut fabric along this fold line to mark the true bias (Figure 1).

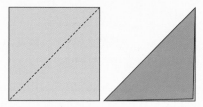

Figure 1

2. Using a clear ruler, mark successive bias lines 1 inch wide. Carefully cut along lines. Handle edges carefully to avoid stretching (Figure 2).

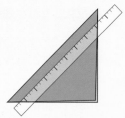

Figure 2

3. Sew short ends of strips together as shown in Figure 3.

Figure 3

4. Fold strip in half lengthwise, wrong sides together. Press.

5. Open out with wrong side up. Fold each edge to center fold and press. Fold in half again and press.

Tankini

Materials

- 2 coordinating fat quarters:
    - 1 print
    - 2 stripe
- ½ yard picot lace trim
- 11 inches ¼-inch-wide elastic
- 1 size-1/0 snap fastener
- Basic sewing supplies and equipment

Cutting

Use pattern templates CC, DD and EE. Transfer pattern markings to fabric pieces.

From print fat quarter:
- Cut two tankini top backs (DD), reversing one.
- Cut one tankini top front (EE) on fold.
- Cut two 1⅞ x 4¼-inch pieces for straps.
- Cut one 2 x 22-inch strip, for waistband and leg bands.

From stripe fat quarter:
- Cut two tankini top backs (DD), reversing one, for lining.
- Cut one tankini top front (EE) on fold for lining.
- Cut four tankini bottoms front/back (CC), reversing two.

Assembly

Stitch with right sides together using ¼-inch seam allowance unless otherwise specified. Refer to General Instructions (page 2) throughout for specific construction techniques.

Tankini Top

1. Sew front to backs at side seams. Repeat with lining pieces.

2. Press and stitch top straps in half lengthwise. Turn right side out. Press flat, centering seam line. Pin straps to top front edge and back top edge along seam line where marked on templates (Figure 1).

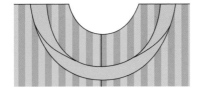

Figure 1

3. Leaving a 2-inch opening along the bottom edge, sew top edges through all layers (Figure 2). Carefully clip curves. Turn to right side through bottom opening and press.

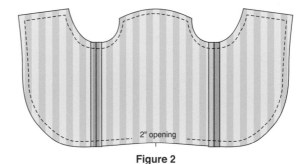

2" opening

Figure 2

House of White Birches, Berne, Indiana 46711   DRGnetwork.com

4. Topstitch picot lace trim to back and bottom edges of tankini top (Figure 3).

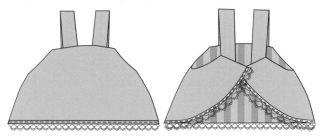

Figure 3

5. Sew snap to top back, lapping left over right.

Tankini Bottoms

1. Stitch bottoms front and back together at side seam. Press seams open. Stitch center front seam (Figure 4). Press seam open.

Figure 4

2. Stitch waistband strip to top edge of bottoms. Trim off excess waistband strip and set aside. Press raw edge under ¼ inch (Figure 5a).

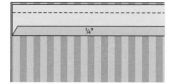

Figure 5a

3. Press under and pin waistband ¾ from seam (Figure 5b). Pin to secure. Topstitch waistband to bottoms creating elastic casing.

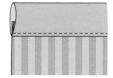

Figure 5b

4. To finish leg edges, press reserved waistband strip (from step 2) in half lengthwise with wrong sides together; cut into two equal lengths. Matching raw edges, pin each strip to tankini leg edges; trim excess length. Stitch through all layers of fabric on both legs (Figure 6a).

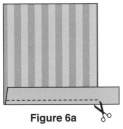

Figure 6a

5. Press strip to wrong side, leaving ⅟₁₆ inch exposed at leg bottom. Topstitch along top edge of strip (Figure 6b).

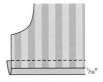

Figure 6b

6. Thread elastic through casing and pin ends of elastic even with bottoms center back seam (Figure 7). Stitch close to raw edges to secure elastic.

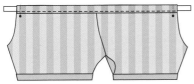

Figure 7

7. Stitch center back seam. Press seam open. Sew inner leg seams to complete tankini bottoms. ❖

Smock Top & Shorts

Materials
- Coordinating fat quarters:
    - 1 stripe
    - 1 solid
- 4 (⅝-inch) buttons
- 2 (11-inch) pieces ¼-inch-wide elastic
- 1 size-1/0 snap fastener
- Basic sewing supplies and equipment

Cutting
Use pattern template L. Transfer pattern markings to fabric pieces.

From stripe fat quarter:
With stripes running vertically:
- Cut one 2½ x 2½-inch square for smock pocket.
- Cut one 8 x 22-inch piece for top bodice.

With stripes running horizontally:
- Cut two 1⅞ x 4¾-inch pieces for top straps.
- Cut two 1 x 6½-inch pieces, for side stripes on shorts.

From solid fat quarter:
- Cut two shorts front and back (L), reversing one.

Assembly
Stitch with right sides together using ¼-inch seam allowances unless otherwise specified. Refer to General Instructions (page 2) throughout for specific construction techniques.

Smock Top
1. Fold and stitch straps lengthwise; turn right side out. Press flat, centering seam line. Topstitch lengthwise ⅛ inch from both edges. Set aside.

2. Using a serger or zigzag stitch, finish one long raw edge of smock-top bodice strip. Press under 1 inch. Topstitch ⅛ inch from finished edge and again ⅜ inch from first stitching to form elastic casing (Figure 1).

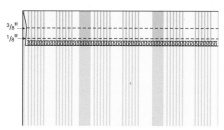

Figure 1

3. Thread elastic through casing. Pin ends of elastic even with ends of smock top; stitch to secure.

4. Stitch a double-turned ¼-inch hem on short edges of smock top and a ¾-inch hem along bottom raw edge.

5. Try smock top on doll, overlapping back opening ¼ inch. Mark placement of shoulder straps with pins (Figure 2). Hand-stitch straps in place along inside edge of smock top at pins.

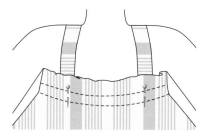

Figure 2

6. On pocket, press under ½ inch along top edge, and ¼ inch along each side and bottom edge. Pin and topstitch pocket onto smock top ¼ inch from bottom, with outer edge of pocket centered below left shoulder strap (Figure 3).

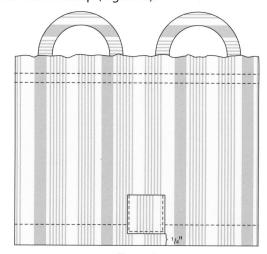

Figure 3

7. Sew a snap to bodice back opening centered on elastic casing, lapping left side over right. Sew buttons to front and back of smock top, centering over shoulder straps at elastic casing.

Shorts

1. Turn under and press ¼ inch along both lengthwise edges of both side strips for shorts.

Referring to side strip placement line on template, center strips on shorts. Topstitch in place close to strip edges (Figure 4).

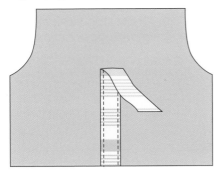

Figure 4

2. Stitch shorts center front seam.

3. Using a serger or zigzag stitch, finish top raw edge of shorts. Press under ½ inch. Stitch ⅜ inch from folded edge to create elastic casing.

4. Thread elastic through casing. Pin ends of elastic even with center back seam of shorts and stitch to secure.

5. Stitch a double-turned ¼-inch hem along shorts-leg bottoms.

6. Stitch center back seam. Press seam open. Sew inner leg seams to complete shorts. ❖

Ruffle Top & Capris

Materials

- Coordinating fat quarters:
    - 1 yellow-with-black print
    - 1 black print
    - 1 black-with-yellow print
- 6½ x 5-inch scrap white fabric for lining
- 11 inches ¼-inch-wide elastic
- 2 size-1/0 sew-on snap fasteners
- Basic sewing supplies and equipment

Cutting

Use pattern templates H, I, O and P. Transfer pattern markings to fabric pieces.

From yellow-with-black print fat quarter:
- Cut two top bodice backs (H), reversing one.
- Cut one top bodice front (I) on fold.
- Cut two 2 x 8-inch pieces for pants-leg cuffs.

From black print fat quarter:
- Cut two capris pants backs (O), reversing one.
- Cut two capris pants fronts (P), reversing one.
- Cut one 1 x 2½-inch piece for front strip.

From black-with-yellow print fat quarter:
- Cut one 3 x 22-inch strip for ruffle.

From white fabric scrap:
- Cut two top bodice backs (H), reversing one, for lining.
- Cut one top bodice front (I) on fold for lining.

Assembly

Stitch right sides together using ¼-inch seam allowance unless otherwise specified. Refer to General Instructions (page 2) throughout for specific construction techniques.

Ruffle Top

1. Press ¼ inch to wrong side along long edges of front strip. Center front strip vertically on bodice front. Topstitch along both sides of strip (Figure 1).

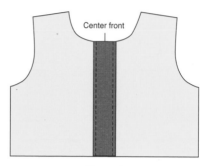

Center front

Figure 1

2. Sew bodice front to backs at shoulder seams. Repeat using white fabric pieces for lining.

3. Sew bodice lining to bodice along center back edges, armholes and neckline (Figure 2).

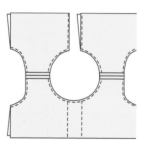

Figure 2

4. Clip curves. Turn right side out and press. Match armhole seams at sides and stitch (Figure 3). Press seams open.

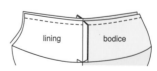

lining   bodice

Figure 3

5. Stitch a double-turned ¼-inch hem on one long edge and both short edges of ruffle strip. Gather raw edge of ruffle and stitch to bodice.

6. Sew snaps to bodice back opening, lapping left over right.

Capris

1. Stitch one pants front and pants back together at side seam (Figure 4). Press seam open. Repeat to make two front/back sections. Stitch center front seam. Press open.

Figure 4

2. Using a serger or zigzag stitch, finish the top raw edge of pants. Press finished edge to wrong side on casing fold line. Topstitch ⅜ inch from folded edge to make casing.

3. Thread elastic through casing. Pin ends of elastic even with back seam and stitch to secure (Figure 5). Stitch pants center back seam. Press open.

Figure 5

4. Press each pants-leg cuff in half lengthwise, wrong sides together. Pin and stitch cuffs to wrong sides of pants-leg bottom edges (Figure 6). Press seams and cuff toward pants. Stitch inner leg seams to complete pants. ❖

Figure 6

Pajama Bunnies

Pajama Bunnies Top

1. Sew shirt fronts and back together at shoulder seams. Press seams open.

2. Press hemline border strips in half lengthwise. Pin one strip along bottom edge of right shirt front. Trim to fit and stitch in place (Figure 1). Press seam toward bodice to create bodice hemline border. Repeat for second shirt front and shirt back. Set aside remaining strip pieces.

Figure 1

3. Construct and stitch collar to shirt neckline (see page 3).

4. Construct and stitch facing to shirt (see page 4).

5. From remaining hemline border strip, cut two lengths to fit sleeve bottoms; set aside remaining strip. Pin and stitch strips to bottoms of sleeves. Press seams toward sleeves.

6. Construct and stitch sleeves to shirt armholes (see page 4). Stitch underarm seams.

7. Sew snaps to front opening, lapping right front over left front.

Pajama Bunnies Pants

1. Stitch two pant-leg sections together at side seam. Press seam open. Repeat with remaining two leg sections. Stitch one center seam (Figure 2). ***Note: Side with sewn center seam will be the pants front.***

Materials
- Coordinating fat quarters:
    1 blue print
    1 pink print
- 1 package ¼-inch coordinating bias tape
- 11 inches ¼-inch-wide elastic
- 6 inches ¼-inch-wide pink satin ribbon
- 2 size-1/0 snap fasteners
- Basic sewing supplies and equipment

Cutting
Use pattern templates C, D, E, G, M and N, following cutting lines for Pajama Bunnies. Transfer pattern markings to fabric pieces.

From blue print:
- Cut one shirt back (C) on fold.
- Cut two shirt fronts (D), reversing one.
- Cut two sleeves (E).
- Cut four pants front and back (M), reversing two.

From pink print:
- Cut two facings (G), reversing one.
- Cut two collars (N) on fold.
- Cut two 2 x 22-inch strips for hemline borders.

Assembly
Stitch right sides together using ¼-inch seam allowance unless otherwise specified. Refer to General Instructions (page 2) throughout for specific constructions techniques.

Figure 2

2. Using a serger or zigzag stitch, finish top raw edge of pants. Press to wrong side along fold line. Stitch ⅜ inch from folded edge to create elastic casing (Figure 3).

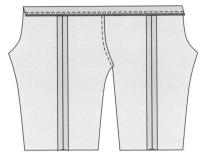

Figure 3

3. Thread elastic through casing. Pin ends of elastic even with center back seams and stitch to secure (Figure 4).

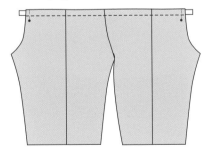

Figure 4

4. Cut remaining hemline border strip to fit bottoms of pants legs. Pin and stitch in place. Press seams toward pants.

5. Stitch center seam on pants back. Press seam open. Stitch inner leg seams.

6. Tie a two-loop bow using satin ribbon. Hand-stitch to waistband center front. ❖

Peasant Dress

Materials
- 1 fat quarter
- 1 package ¼-inch coordinating bias tape
- ⅔ yard white mini ball fringe
- 1¾ yards ¾-inch-wide printed grosgrain ribbon
- 24 inches ¼-inch-wide elastic
- Basic sewing supplies and equipment

Cutting
Use pattern templates Q and R. Transfer pattern markings to fabric pieces.

From fat quarter:
- Cut two peasant dress front/backs (Q), reversing one.
- Cut two peasant dress sleeves (R) on fold.

From elastic:
- Cut two 5-inch lengths for sleeves.
- Cut one 11-inch length for neckline.

From bias tape:
- Cut one 20-inch length for neckline binding.

Assembly
Stitch right sides together using ¼-inch seam allowances unless otherwise specified. Refer to General Instructions (page 2) throughout for specific construction techniques.

1. Stitch sleeves to armholes of dress front and back (Figure 1).

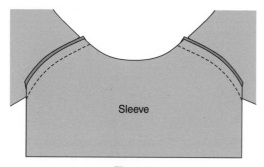

Figure 1

2. Press under ¼ inch on bottom edge of each sleeve. Press under again on casing fold line. Topstitch close to first folded edge and again ¼ inch from casing fold line to make casing for elastic (Figure 2).

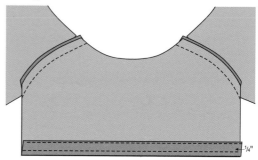

Figure 2

3. Thread 5-inch lengths of elastic through sleeve casings. Pin ends of elastic to sleeve edges and stitch to secure. Stitch underarm and side seams of dress.

4. Press open center fold of 20-inch length of bias tape. Cut piece long enough to fit around neckline, allowing ½ inch extra. Press under raw edge of beginning end ¼ inch. Stitch bias tape to neckline of peasant dress, overlapping ends (Figure 3).

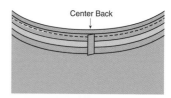

Figure 3

5. Press bias tape to wrong side of dress neckline. Edgestitch bottom edge of bias tape to dress from center back to within 2 inches of center back (Figure 4).

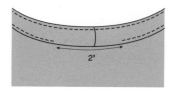

Figure 4

6. Thread 11-inch length of elastic through casing. Overlap elastic ends ½ inch and stitch to secure (Figure 5). Stitch 2-inch opening closed, keeping elastic free of stitching.

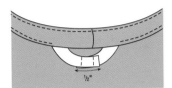

Figure 5

7. Using a serger or zigzag stitch, finish bottom raw edge of peasant dress. Beginning at side seam, pin mini ball fringe to right side of dress bottom, covering serger/zigzag stitching (Figure 6). Trim length of fringe to meet at side seam. Stitch.

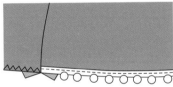

Figure 6

8. Pin grosgrain ribbon over mini ball trim, overlapping ends ½ inch at side seam. Turn under raw end ¼ inch and then topstitch both edges of ribbon (Figure 7). Repeat with additional piece of grosgrain ribbon, positioning ¾ inch above top edge of first ribbon piece.

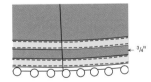

Figure 7

9. Cut remaining ribbon length in half. Tie two 2-loop bows, trimming ends diagonally. Hand-stitch bows to ribbon trim on front , referring to photo for placement. ❖

Wrap Dress

Materials
- 2 coordinating fat quarters
- Scrap white cotton fabric
- 1 package ¼-inch coordinating bias tape
- Decorative button
- 2 size-1/0 snap fasteners
- Basic sewing supplies and equipment

Cutting
Use pattern templates S, T and U. Transfer pattern markings to fabric pieces.

From first fat quarter:
- Cut one wrap dress bodice back (S) on fold.
- Cut one wrap dress bodice left front (T).
- Cut one wrap dress bodice right front (U).
- Cut one 26 x 6½-inch piece for skirt.

From second fat quarter:
- Cut one 1½ x 13-inch strip for waistband.

From scrap cotton fabric:
- Cut one wrap dress bodice back (S) on fold for lining.
- Cut one wrap dress bodice left front (T) for lining.
- Cut one wrap dress bodice right front (U) for lining.
- Cut one 1½ x 13-inch strip for waistband for lining.

Assembly
Stitch with right sides together, using a ¼-inch seam unless otherwise specified. Refer to General Instructions (page 2) throughout for specific construction techniques.

1. Sew bodice fronts to bodice back at shoulder seams. Press seams open. Repeat with bodice fronts and back lining.

2. Sew bodice lining to bodice at front edges, neckline and armholes (Figure 1).

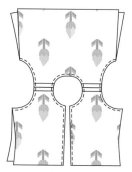

Figure 1

3. Clip curves, turn right side out and press. Match armhole seams at sides and stitch (Figure 2). Press seams open.

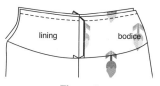

Figure 2

4. Stitch short ends of waistband and waistband lining together. Pin bodice between waistband and waistband lining, with bodice and waistband right

Folding Pleats
1. Mark pleats on wrong side of fabric (Figure 1).

Figure 1

2. With top edge facing you, fold pleats by bringing marked pleat lines together. Pin pleat with fold to the right (Figure 2). Press.

Figure 2

3. Baste across pleats at seam line to secure (Figure 3). Remove basting after stitching.

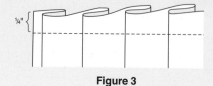

Figure 3

sides together (Figure 3). Stitch through all thicknesses. Turn waistband right side out. Press.

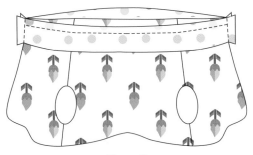

Figure 3

5. Mark 1-inch intervals across the top edge of skirt and pleat (see Folding Pleats on facing page). Pin waistband to top edge of skirt, matching front edges and keeping waistband lining free (Figure 4). *Note: If skirt does not match waistband length, adjust pleats accordingly.*

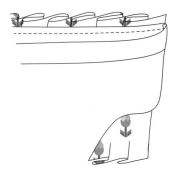

Figure 4

6. Turn under ¼ inch along waistband lining. Handstitch at skirt stitching line to secure (Figure 5).

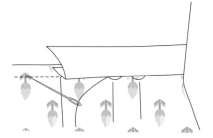

Figure 5

7. Apply bias tape to dress front and neckline edges. Make a 1-inch hem on skirt.

8. Sew snaps to waistband, lapping right front over left front. Sew decorative button to waistband, centered on waistband on right front edge. ❖

Sundress & Bolero Jacket

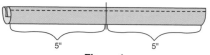

Figure 1

2. Sew one sundress bodice front to two bodice back sections at side seams (Figure 2). Repeat with second set of bodice sections to make lining.

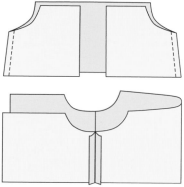

Figure 2

3. Pin ends of shoulder straps to front and back edges of bodice as indicated on pattern templates (Figure 3).

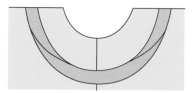

Figure 3

4. Sew bodice lining to sundress bodice at center back edges, bodice top and armholes (Figure 4). Clip curves, turn right side out and press.

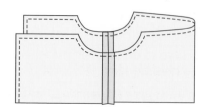

Figure 4

Materials
- 2 coordinating fat quarters
- 1 package ¼-inch coordinating bias tape
- 3 (⅜- to ½-inch) buttons
- 3 size-1/0 snap fasteners
- Basic sewing supplies and equipment

Cutting
Use pattern templates V, W, X, Y, Z, AA and BB. Transfer pattern markings to fabric pieces.

From first fat quarter:
- Cut two sundress bodice fronts (Z) on fold for bodice and lining.
- Cut four sundress bodice backs (Y), reversing two, for bodice and lining.
- Cut one sundress skirt front (BB) on fold.
- Cut two sundress skirt backs (AA), reversing one.

From second fat quarter:
- Cut 1 bolero jacket back (V) on fold.
- Cut two bolero jacket fronts (W), reversing one.
- Cut two bolero jacket sleeves (X).

From bias tape:
- Cut 1 (10-inch) length for shoulder straps.

Assembly
Stitch right sides together using ¼-inch seam allowances unless otherwise specified. Refer to General Instructions (page 2) throughout for specific construction techniques.

Sundress
1. Topstitch edges of 10-inch shoulder-strap bias tape together. Cut to make two 5-inch shoulder straps (Figure 1). Set aside.

5. Sew center back seam of sundress skirt from dot to skirt bottom. Press seam allowance open from top to bottom. Topstitch both sides of seam allowance (Figure 5).

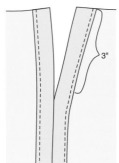

Figure 5

6. Stitch darts at sundress skirt front (Figure 6). Press darts toward center front. Stitch skirt front and back together at side seams.

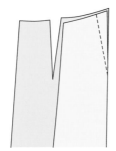

Figure 6

7. Stitch skirt to bodice, matching side seams and aligning center back edges. Press seam toward skirt. Hem sundress bottom edge ¼ inch.

8. Sew two snaps to back opening at top and bottom of bodice, lapping left over right. Sew two buttons to front of sundress on tops of straps.

Bolero Jacket

1. Sew bolero jacket front and backs together at shoulder seams. Press seams open. Set aside.

2. Apply bias tape to bottom edges of sleeves. Stitch sleeves to jacket. Stitch underarm seam.

3. Apply bias tape to all edges of jacket bodice.

4. Sew snap at top of jacket front opening, lapping right front over left front. Sew button to jacket front over snap. ❖

Garment Accessories

4. Edgestitch along both ends of hair band through all layers (Figure 2).

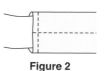

Figure 2

5. Embellish hair band as desired by hand-stitching flowers, bows or buttons to center front (Figure 3).

Figure 3

Hair Band

Materials
- Scrap fabric to match garment
- 3 inches 1-inch-wide elastic
- Embellishment (button, ribbon bow or flower)
- Basic sewing supplies and equipment

Cutting
From scrap fabric:
- Cut one 10¼ x 2½-inch piece.

Assembly
Stitch right sides together using ¼-inch seam allowance unless otherwise specified.

1. Press ¼ inch to wrong side on both short ends of hair band.

2. Press hair band in half lengthwise with right sides together. Stitch long edges together. Turn right side out and press flat, centering seam on back.

3. Insert elastic into open ends of hair band and pin (Figure 1). *Note: Try hair band on doll and adjust length of elastic as needed to fit.*

Figure 1

Purse

Materials
- 2 coordinating scraps fabric to match garment
- 2 (1½ inch) metal D-rings
- Decorative button
- Basic sewing supplies and equipment

Cutting
Use pattern template FF.

From first coordinating scrap fabric:
- Cut 2 purse front and back (FF) on fold.

From second coordinating scrap fabric:
- Cut 2 purse front and back (FF) on fold, for lining.

Assembly
Stitch right sides together using a ¼-inch seam allowance unless otherwise specified.

1. Stitch across side and bottom edges of purse front and back. Repeat with lining front and back (Figure 4).

Figure 4

2. Turn purse fabric sections right side out and finger-press.

3. Insert purse into lining, right sides together. Stitch together at curve (Figure 5).

Figure 5

4. Clip curves and turn purse lining to inside of purse, aligning top edges.

5. Using a serger or a zigzag stitch, sew across top edges of purse through all layers (Figure 6).

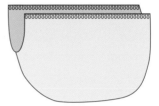

Figure 6

6. Lay one D-ring across top edge of one purse side. Turn edge over ring, hand-stitching to inside of purse as you turn (Figure 7). Repeat for opposite side of purse.

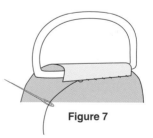

Figure 7

7. Sew a decorative button to front of purse (Figure 8). ❖

Figure 8

Short-Sleeve Blouse & Wrap Skirt

Materials
- 2 coordinating fat quarters:
    - 1 polka dot
    - 1 print
- 1 package ¼-inch coordinating bias tape
- 1 yard picot-edge trim
- Four ½-inch buttons
- 4 size-1/0 snap fasteners
- Basic sewing supplies and equipment

Cutting
Use pattern templates C, D, E, G and N, using cutting lines for Short-Sleeve Blouse. Transfer pattern markings to fabric pieces.

From polka dot fat quarter:
- Cut two blouse fronts (D), reversing one.
- Cut one blouse back (C) on fold.
- Cut two sleeves (E).
- Cut two collars (N) on fold.
- Cut two facings (G), reversing one.
- Cut two 2 x 22-inch pieces for skirt hemline border.

From print fat quarter:
- Cut two 13½ x 6½-inch piece for skirt.
- Cut one 1½ x 13½-inch strip for skirt waistband.

Assembly
Stitch with right sides together, using ¼-inch seam allowances unless otherwise specified. Refer to General Instructions (page 2) throughout for specific constructions techniques.

Short-Sleeve Blouse
1. Sew blouse fronts and back together at shoulder seams. Press seams open.

2. Stitch collar pieces together (see page 3). Apply picot-edge trim close to curved collar edge (Figure 1). Sew collar to neckline. Construct facing and apply to blouse (see page 4).

Figure 1

3. Hem bottom edge of each sleeve ¼ inch. Pin and stitch picot-edge trim over sleeve hemline stitching (Figure 2). Sew sleeves into blouse armholes (see page 4).

Figure 2

4. Hem bottom of blouse ¼ inch. Evenly space and sew snaps to blouse front, lapping right front over left front.

Wrap Skirt
1. Sew hemline border strips together at short ends. Press seam open. Press hemline border strip in half lengthwise, wrong sides together.

2. Stitch skirt sections together at center back (6½-inch edges). Press seam open. Stitch hem border strip to skirt bottom edge, matching seams at back. Trim ends of strip even with skirt. Press seam toward skirt.

3. Stitch double-turned ¼-inch hem in skirt front edges (Figure 3). Mark 1-inch intervals across the top edge of skirt and pleat (see Folding Pleats on page 22).

Figure 3

4. Fold waistband in half lengthwise. Stitch short ends together. Turn right side out and press.

Pin raw edge of one side of waistband to skirt top, matching front edges (Figure 4). ***Note:*** *If skirt does not match waistband length, adjust pleats to match.*

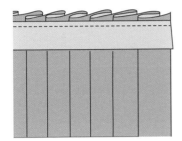

Figure 4

5. Fold waistband to wrong side of skirt over seam. Turn waistband under and hand-stitch to secure (Figure 5).

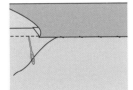

Figure 5

6. Sew snaps to waistband at edge and 2 inches from the edge, lapping right front over left front. Sew two buttons to waistband front, positioning over snaps. Sew two buttons down skirt right front, spacing approximately 1½ inches apart (Figure 6). ❖

Figure 6

House of White Birches, Berne, Indiana 46711 DRGnetwork.com

Bell-Sleeve Jacket & Skirt

Assembly

Stitch right sides together using ¼-inch seam allowances unless otherwise specified. Refer to General Instructions (page 2) throughout for specific constructions techniques.

Bell-Sleeve Jacket

1. Sew jacket fronts and back together at shoulder seams. Press seams open. Construct facings and stitch to jacket (see page 4).

2. For each sleeve ruffle, press 10½ x 2⅞-inch piece in half lengthwise with wrong sides together. Gather raw edge to fit bottom edge of sleeve. Stitch ruffle to sleeve (Figure 1). Press seam toward sleeve. Complete sleeve construction and stitch sleeves to jacket.

Figure 1

3. Make ¼-inch hem on jacket bottom. Sew on snaps, positioning 1¾ inches from neckline and 1¼ inches apart, lapping right front over left front (Figure 2).

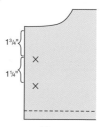

1¾"

1¼"

Figure 2

4. Sew buttons over snaps. If desired, press right corner lapel of jacket back to reveal contrasting facing fabric.

Materials

- 2 coordinating fat quarters:
    1 check
    1 print
- 1 package coordinating ¼-inch bias tape
- 6 (½-inch) buttons
- One ¼ x 11-inch piece elastic
- 2 size-1/0 snap fasteners
- Basic sewing supplies and equipment

Cutting

Use pattern templates C, D, E and G, following cutting lines for Bell-Sleeve Jacket. Transfer pattern markings to fabric pieces.

From check fat quarter:
- Cut two jacket fronts (D), reversing one.
- Cut one jacket back (C) on fold.
- Cut two sleeves (E).
- Cut two 10½ x 2⅞-inch pieces for sleeve ruffles.
- Cut two 2 x 18-inch pieces for skirt ruffle.

From print fat quarter:
- Cut two facings (G), reversing one.
- Cut one 6 x 18-inch piece for skirt.

Skirt

1. Stitch together 2 x 18-inch skirt ruffle pieces at one short edge. Press seam open. Fold piece in half lengthwise, wrong sides together. Beginning ½ inch from one end of ruffle, mark 1-inch intervals across ruffle (Figure 3). Pleat ruffle (see Folding Pleats on page 22).

Figure 3

2. Pin pleated ruffle to skirt bottom edge, trimming excess ruffle length, or adjusting pleats as needed (Figure 4). Stitch ruffle to skirt. Press seam toward skirt. Topstitch ruffle seam allowance to skirt.

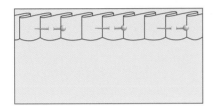

Figure 4

3. Using a serger or a zigzag stitch, finish top raw edge of skirt. Press finished edge ½ inch to wrong side. Stitch ⅜ inch from folded edge to create casing for elastic.

4. Thread elastic through casing. Pin ends of elastic even with skirt edges and stitch to secure.

5. Stitch short edges of skirt together creating center front seam. Press seam open.

6. Topstitch along both sides of seam. Position four buttons evenly spaced along center front seam between elastic casing and ruffle seam (Figure 5). ❖

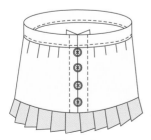

Figure 5

House of White Birches, Berne, Indiana 46711 DRGnetwork.com

Bubble Sundress

Materials
- 2 coordinating fat quarters:
    - 1 polka dot
    - 1 print
- 2 (½-inch) buttons
- 2 size-1/0 snap fasteners
- Basic sewing supplies and equipment

Cutting
Use pattern templates GG and HH. Transfer pattern markings to fabric pieces.

From polka dot fat quarter:
- Cut one bubble sundress bodice front (HH) on fold, for lining.
- Cut two bubble sundress bodice backs (GG), reversing one, for lining.
- Cut one 2¾ x 2½-inch piece for pocket.
- Cut two 7 x 8½-inch pieces for skirt backs.
- Cut one 7 x 14-inch section for skirt front.

From print fat quarter:
- Cut one bubble sundress bodice front (HH) on fold.
- Cut two bubble sundress bodice backs (GG), reversing one.
- Cut one 2¾ x 1½-inch piece for pocket trim.
- Cut two 2 x 14-inch strips for hemline bands.
- Cut one 2 x 22-inch strip for straps and bow.

Assembly
Stitch with right sides together using ¼-inch seam allowances unless otherwise specified. Refer to General Instructions (page 2) throughout for specific construction techniques.

1. Fold the 2 x 14-inch print strip for straps and bow right sides together, matching long edges. Stitch long edges; turn right side out and press flat, centering the seam line. Cut two 5-inch lengths from the strip for straps. Tie remaining length into a bow, trimming ends diagonally. Set bow aside.

2. Sew bodice front to bodice backs at side seams. Repeat with bodice lining pieces.

3. Position and pin straps as indicated on bodice pattern templates (Figure 1).

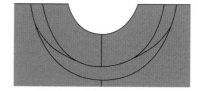

Figure 1

4. Sew lining to sundress bodice along center back, neckline and armholes (Figure 2). Carefully clip curves. Turn right side out and press.

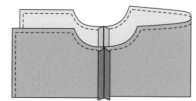

Figure 2

5. Sew skirt back pieces together, leaving a 3-inch opening at the top. Press seam allowances open and topstitch down both sides of the seam (Figure 3). Sew skirt back to front at side seams. Press seams open.

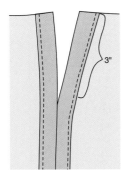

Figure 3

6. Press pocket trim in half lengthwise with wrong side together. Stitch pocket trim to top edge of pocket, matching raw edges. Press. Turn under ¼ inch along sides and bottom edges of pocket. Press. Sew a button to center front of pocket.

7. Place pocket 2 inches below top of skirt and 2½ inches from side seam. Topstitch along sides and bottom edge of pocket.

8. Stitch short edges of 2 x 22-inch print strips together to form the hemline band. Press seams open. Press in half lengthwise with wrong sides together. Cut the hemline band the length of the circumference of the skirt bottom edge plus ½ inch for seam allowance. Stitch short edges right sides together, press seam open and refold in half lengthwise. Pin and stitch band to bottom of sundress with raw edges even. Press seam toward skirt.

9. Gather top edge of skirt to fit bodice. Stitch skirt to bodice with right sides together, matching raw edges. Press seam toward skirt.

10. Sew bow made earlier to center front bodice. Sew snaps to top and bottom of bodice back, lapping left over right. Sew button over snap at bottom left of bodice back at bodice/skirt seam line. ❖

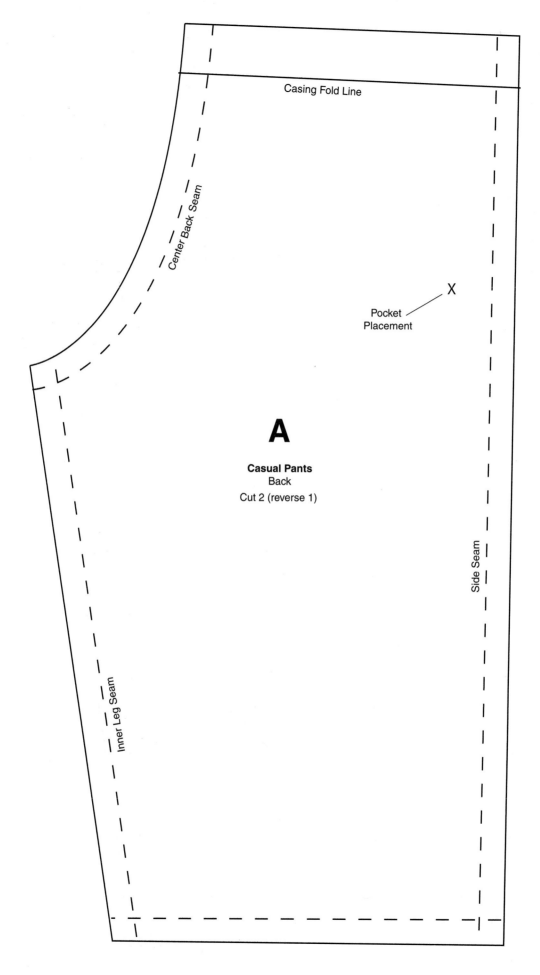

Casing Fold Line

Center Back Seam

X

Pocket
Placement

A

Casual Pants
Back
Cut 2 (reverse 1)

Side Seam

Inner Leg Seam

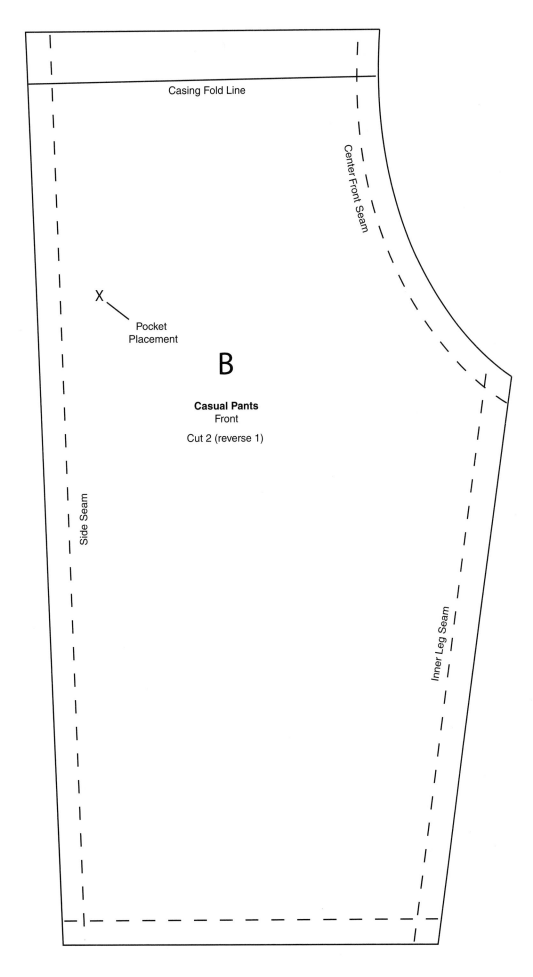

Casing Fold Line

Center Front Seam

X

Pocket
Placement

B

Casual Pants
Front

Cut 2 (reverse 1)

Side Seam

Inner Leg Seam

House of White Birches, Berne, Indiana 46711   DRGnetwork.com

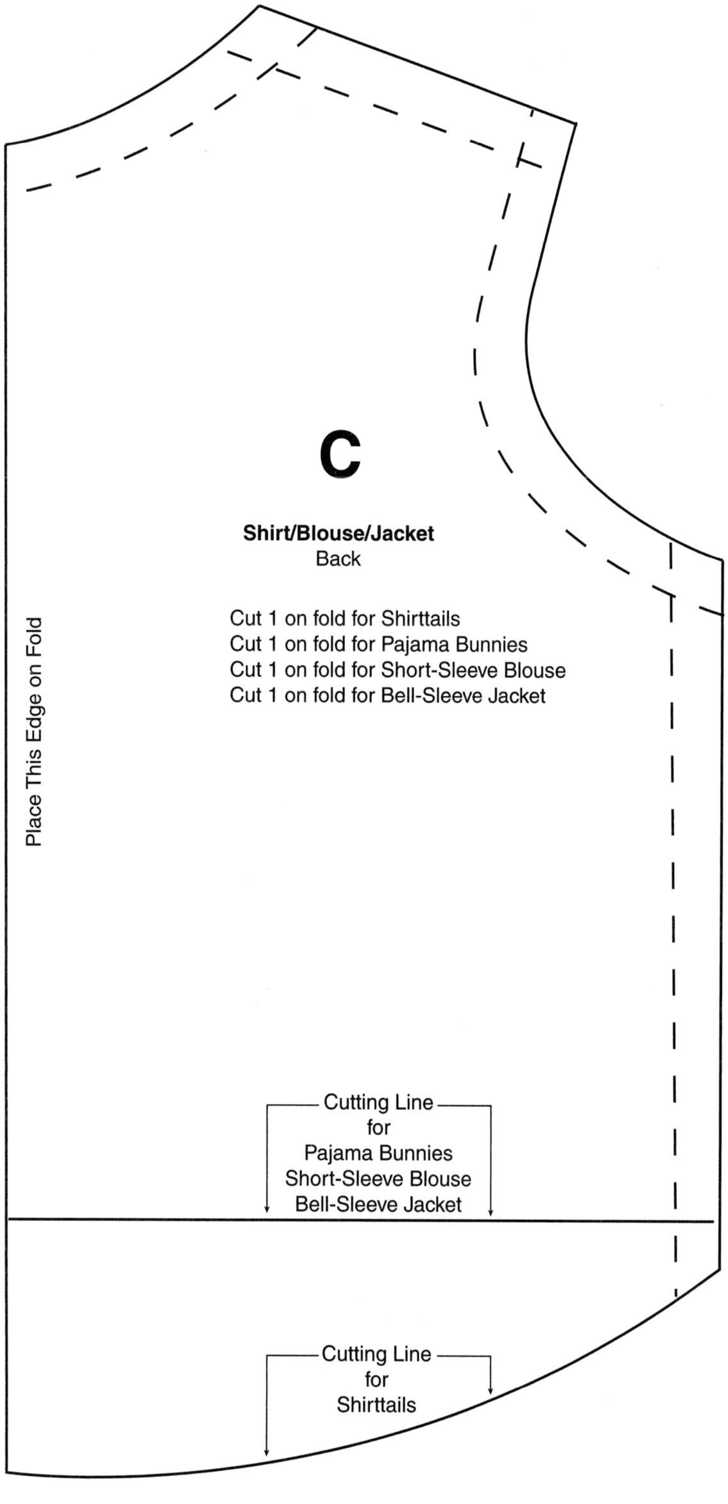

C

Shirt/Blouse/Jacket
Back

Cut 1 on fold for Shirttails
Cut 1 on fold for Pajama Bunnies
Cut 1 on fold for Short-Sleeve Blouse
Cut 1 on fold for Bell-Sleeve Jacket

Place This Edge on Fold

Cutting Line
for
Pajama Bunnies
Short-Sleeve Blouse
Bell-Sleeve Jacket

Cutting Line
for
Shirttails

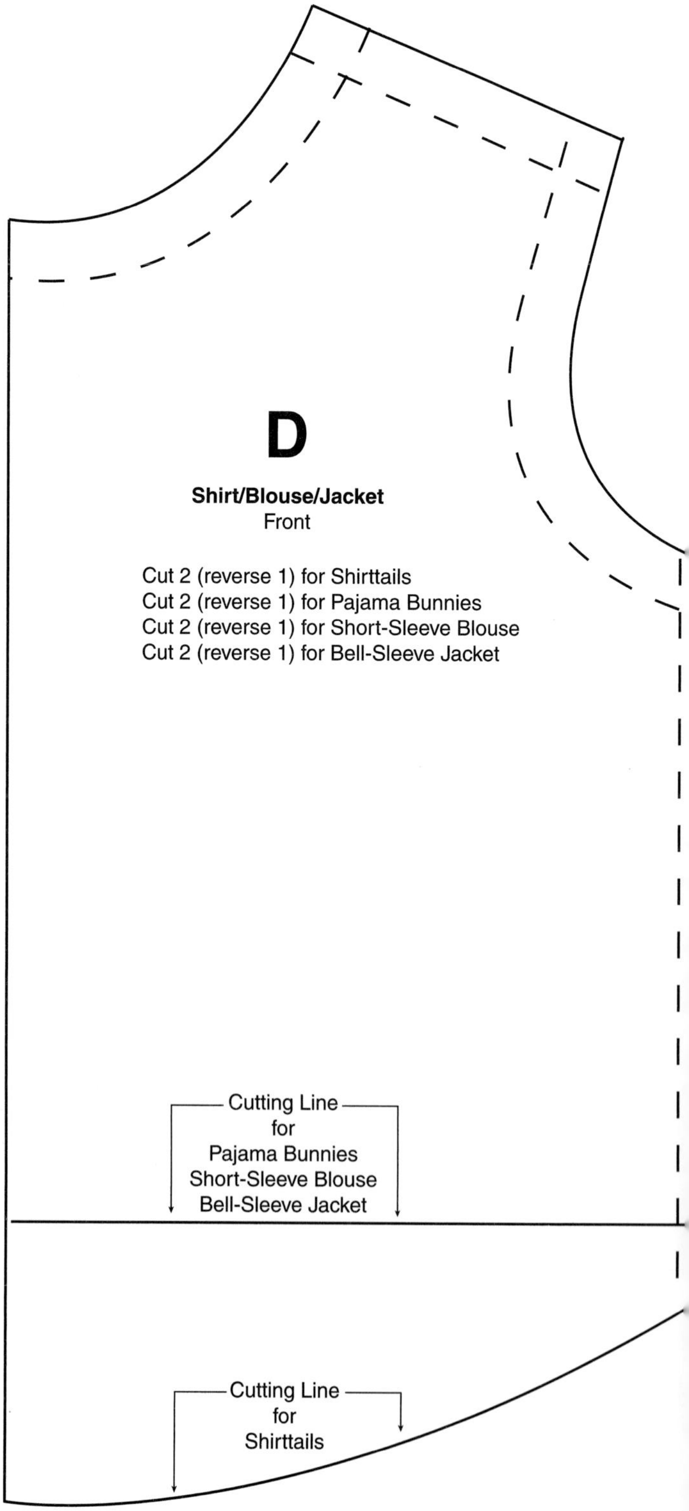

D

Shirt/Blouse/Jacket
Front

Cut 2 (reverse 1) for Shirttails
Cut 2 (reverse 1) for Pajama Bunnies
Cut 2 (reverse 1) for Short-Sleeve Blouse
Cut 2 (reverse 1) for Bell-Sleeve Jacket

Cutting Line
for
Pajama Bunnies
Short-Sleeve Blouse
Bell-Sleeve Jacket

Cutting Line
for
Shirttails

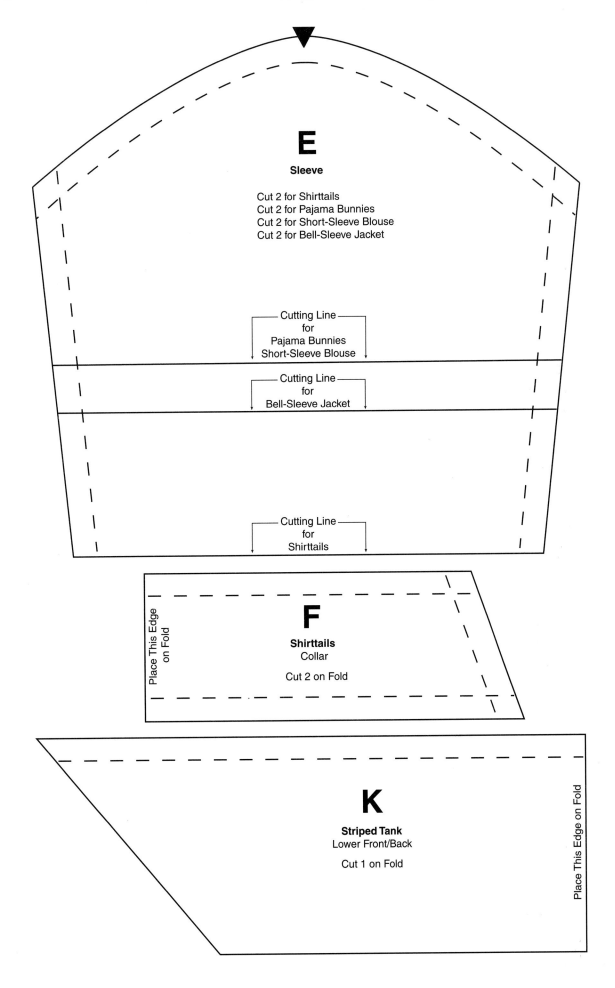

E

Sleeve

Cut 2 for Shirttails
Cut 2 for Pajama Bunnies
Cut 2 for Short-Sleeve Blouse
Cut 2 for Bell-Sleeve Jacket

Cutting Line
for
Pajama Bunnies
Short-Sleeve Blouse

Cutting Line
for
Bell-Sleeve Jacket

Cutting Line
for
Shirttails

F

Shirttails
Collar

Cut 2 on Fold

Place This Edge on Fold

K

Striped Tank
Lower Front/Back

Cut 1 on Fold

Place This Edge on Fold

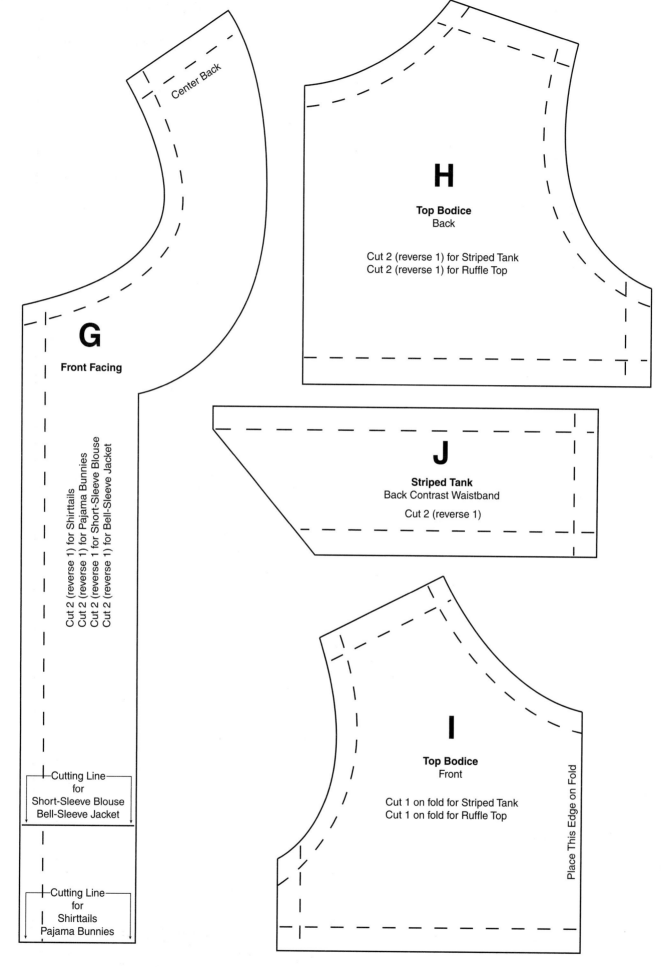

Center Back

G

Front Facing

Cut 2 (reverse 1) for Shirttails
Cut 2 (reverse 1) for Pajama Bunnies
Cut 2 (reverse 1) for Short-Sleeve Blouse
Cut 2 (reverse 1) for Bell-Sleeve Jacket

Cutting Line
for
Short-Sleeve Blouse
Bell-Sleeve Jacket

Cutting Line
for
Shirttails
Pajama Bunnies

H

Top Bodice
Back

Cut 2 (reverse 1) for Striped Tank
Cut 2 (reverse 1) for Ruffle Top

J

Striped Tank
Back Contrast Waistband

Cut 2 (reverse 1)

I

Top Bodice
Front

Cut 1 on fold for Striped Tank
Cut 1 on fold for Ruffle Top

Place This Edge on Fold

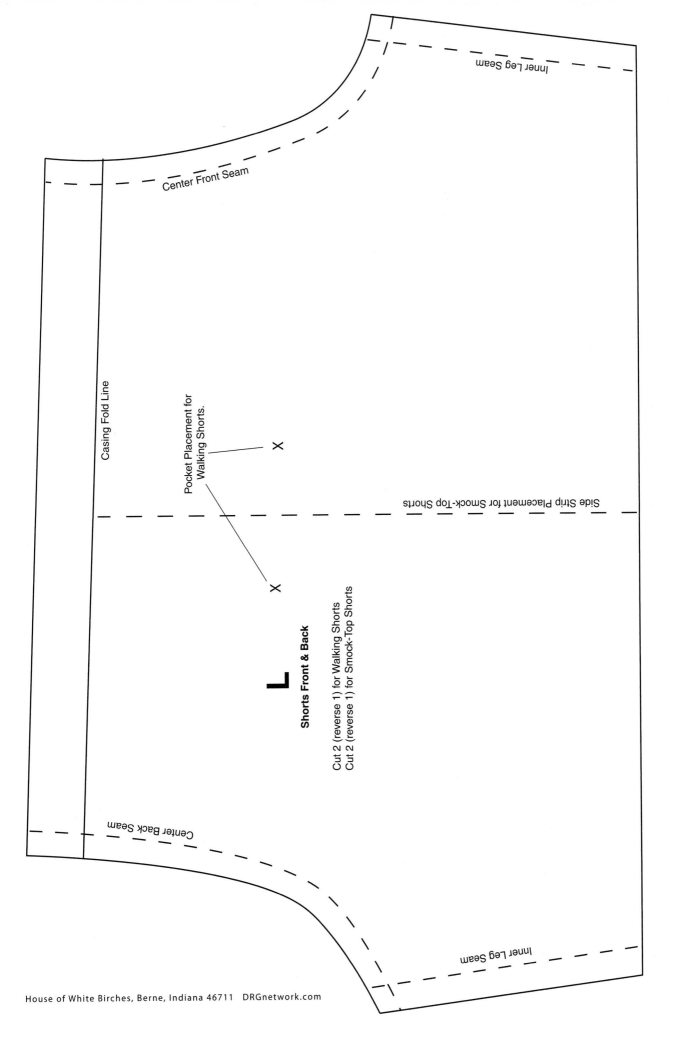

Inner Leg Seam

Center Front Seam

Casing Fold Line

Pocket Placement for Walking Shorts.

Side Strip Placement for Smock-Top Shorts

X

X

Shorts Front & Back

Cut 2 (reverse 1) for Walking Shorts
Cut 2 (reverse 1) for Smock-Top Shorts

Inner Leg Seam

Center Back Seam

Inner Leg Seam

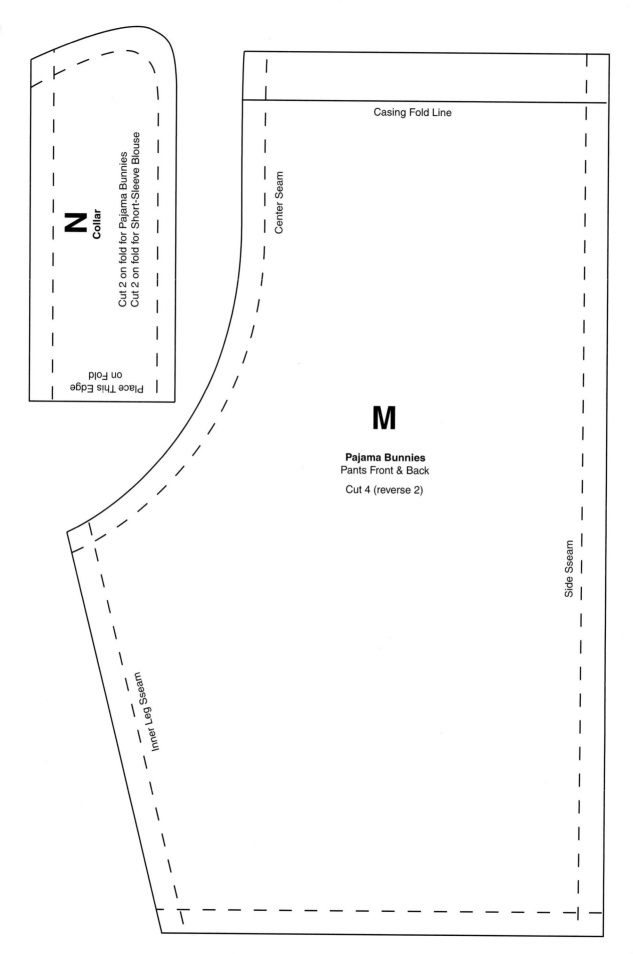

N

Collar

Cut 2 on fold for Pajama Bunnies
Cut 2 on fold for Short-Sleeve Blouse

Place This Edge
on Fold

Casing Fold Line

Center Seam

M

Pajama Bunnies
Pants Front & Back

Cut 4 (reverse 2)

Side Sseam

Inner Leg Sseam

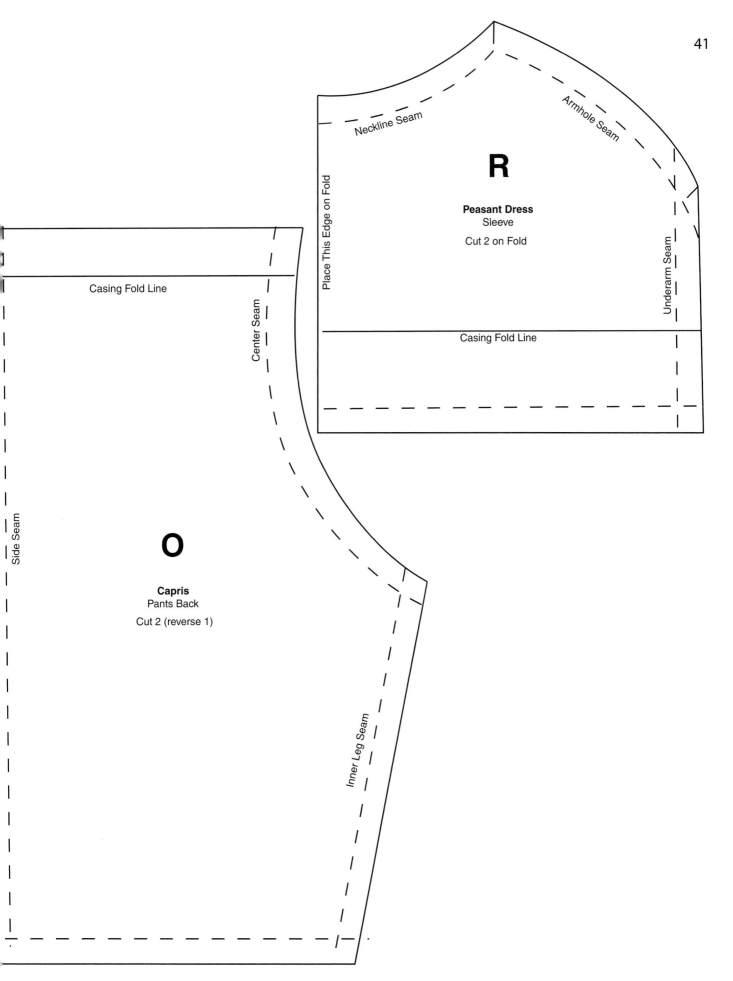

R

Peasant Dress
Sleeve
Cut 2 on Fold

Neckline Seam

Armhole Seam

Place This Edge on Fold

Underarm Seam

Casing Fold Line

Casing Fold Line

Center Seam

Side Seam

O

Capris
Pants Back
Cut 2 (reverse 1)

Inner Leg Seam

House of White Birches, Berne, Indiana 46711   DRGnetwork.com

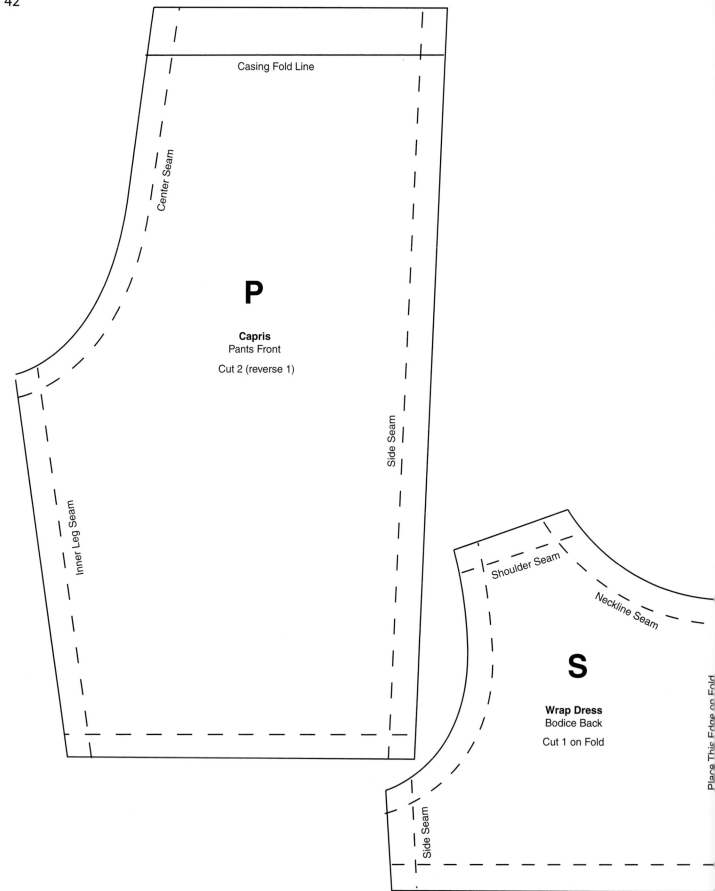

Casing Fold Line

Center Seam

P

Capris
Pants Front

Cut 2 (reverse 1)

Side Seam

Inner Leg Seam

Shoulder Seam

Neckline Seam

S

Wrap Dress
Bodice Back

Cut 1 on Fold

Side Seam

Place This Edge on Fold

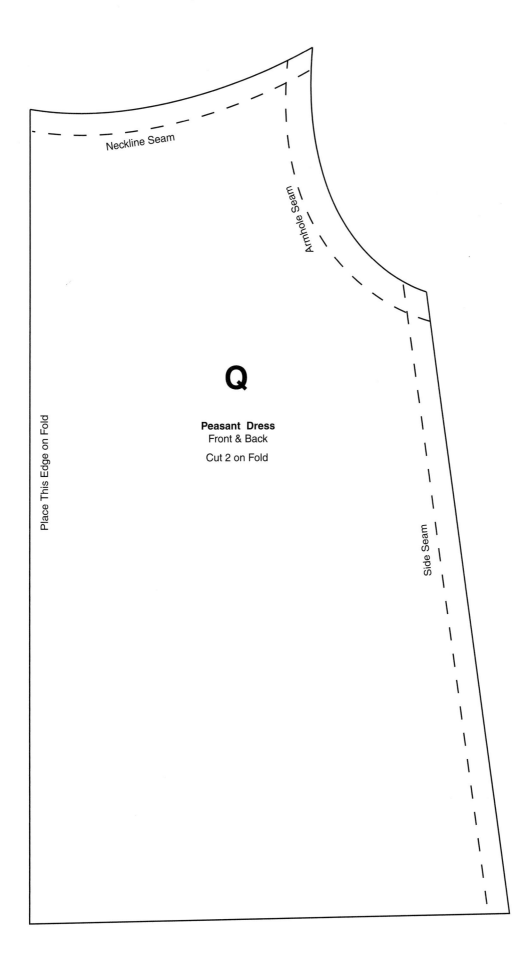

Neckline Seam

Armhole Seam

Place This Edge on Fold

Q

Peasant Dress
Front & Back

Cut 2 on Fold

Side Seam

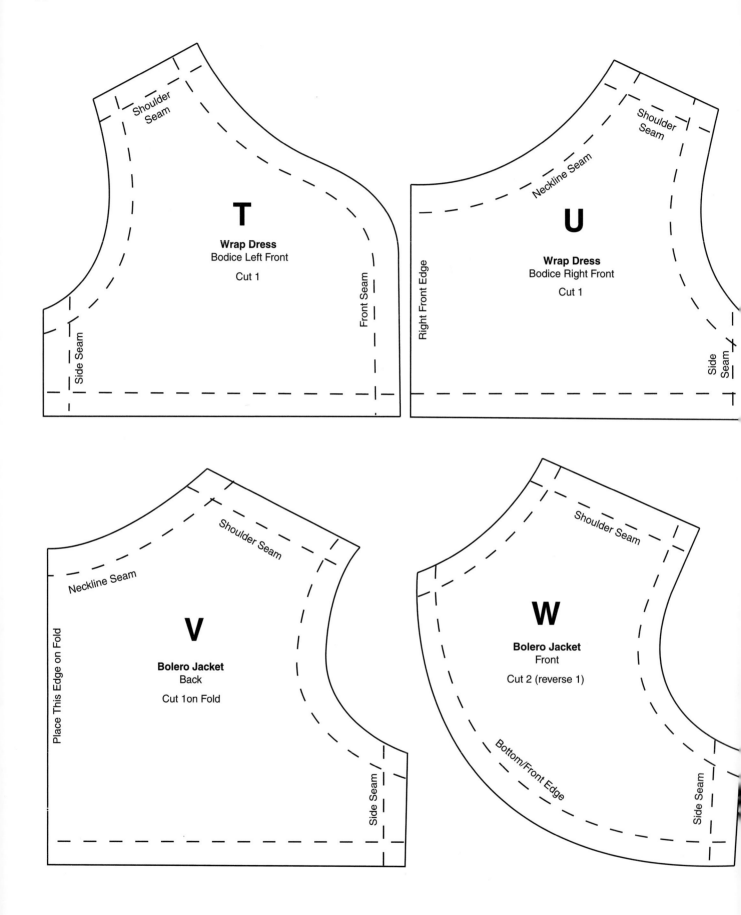

T

Wrap Dress
Bodice Left Front

Cut 1

Shoulder Seam

Side Seam

Front Seam

U

Wrap Dress
Bodice Right Front

Cut 1

Neckline Seam

Shoulder Seam

Right Front Edge

Side Seam

V

Bolero Jacket
Back

Cut 1 on Fold

Neckline Seam

Shoulder Seam

Place This Edge on Fold

Side Seam

W

Bolero Jacket
Front

Cut 2 (reverse 1)

Shoulder Seam

Bottom/Front Edge

Side Seam

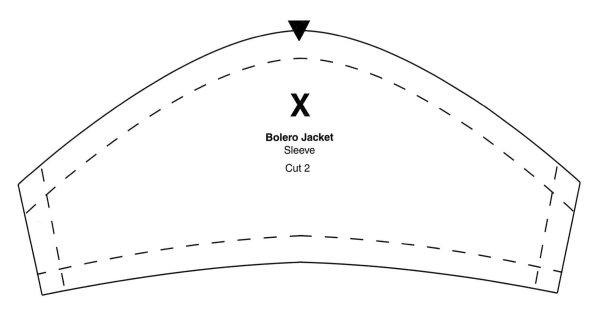

X
Bolero Jacket
Sleeve
Cut 2

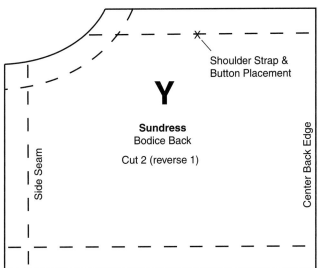

Y
Sundress
Bodice Back
Cut 2 (reverse 1)

Shoulder Strap &
Button Placement

Side Seam

Center Back Edge

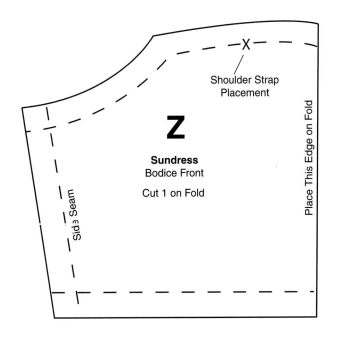

Z
Sundress
Bodice Front
Cut 1 on Fold

Shoulder Strap
Placement

Side Seam

Place This Edge on Fold

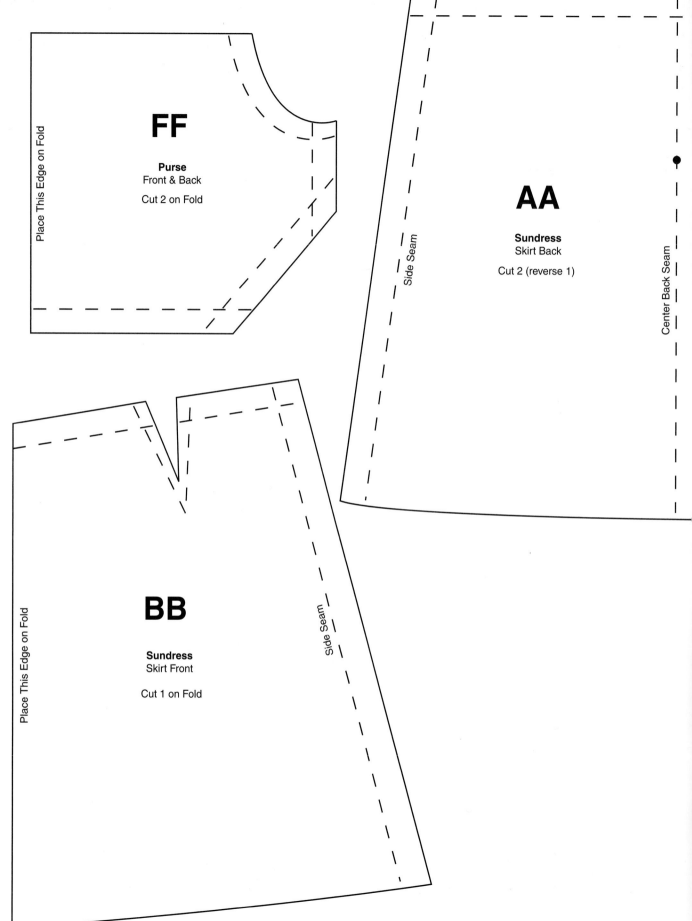

FF

Purse
Front & Back

Cut 2 on Fold

Place This Edge on Fold

AA

Sundress
Skirt Back

Cut 2 (reverse 1)

Side Seam

Center Back Seam

BB

Sundress
Skirt Front

Cut 1 on Fold

Place This Edge on Fold

Side Seam

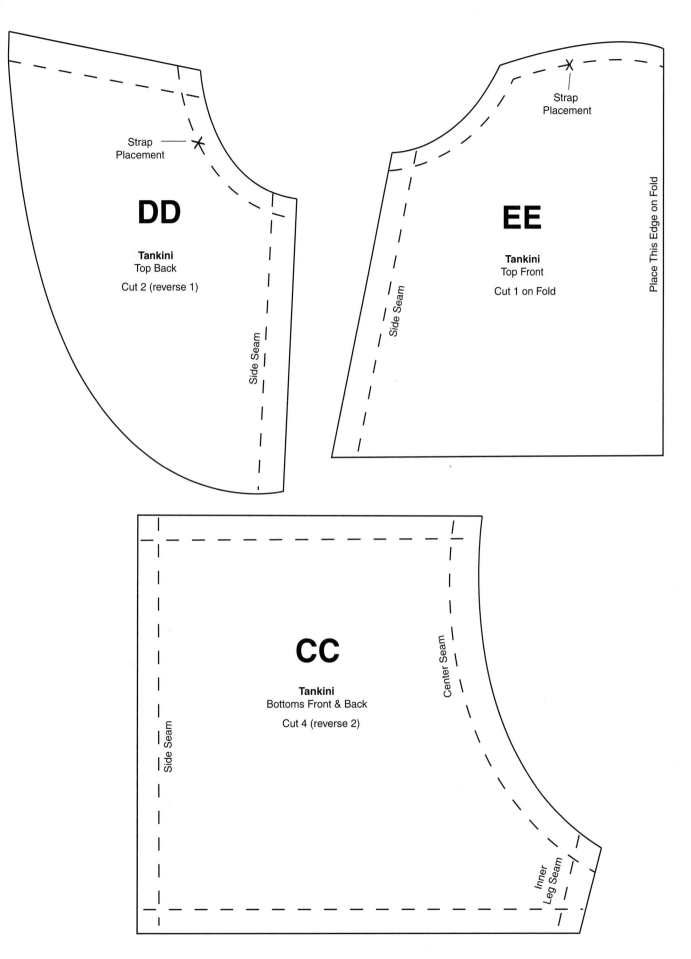

DD

Tankini
Top Back

Cut 2 (reverse 1)

Strap Placement

Side Seam

EE

Tankini
Top Front

Cut 1 on Fold

Strap Placement

Side Seam

Place This Edge on Fold

CC

Tankini
Bottoms Front & Back

Cut 4 (reverse 2)

Side Seam

Center Seam

Inner Leg Seam

House of White Birches, Berne, Indiana 46711   DRGnetwork.com

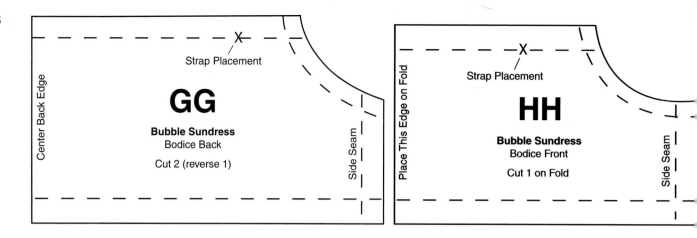

GG

Bubble Sundress
Bodice Back

Cut 2 (reverse 1)

Center Back Edge

Strap Placement

Side Seam

HH

Bubble Sundress
Bodice Front

Cut 1 on Fold

Place This Edge on Fold

Strap Placement

Side Seam

Metric Conversion Charts

Metric Conversions

yards	x	.9144	=	metres (m)
yards	x	91.44	=	centimetres (cm)
inches	x	2.54	=	centimetres (cm)
inches	x	25.40	=	millimetres (mm)
inches	x	.0254	=	metres (m)

centimetres	x	.3937	=	inches
metres	x	1.0936	=	yards

Standard Equivalents

⅛ inch	=	3.20mm	=	0.32cm
¼ inch	=	6.35mm	=	0.635cm
⅜ inch	=	9.50mm	=	0.95cm
½ inch	=	12.70mm	=	1.27cm
⅝ inch	=	15.90mm	=	1.59cm
¾ inch	=	19.10mm	=	1.91cm
⅞ inch	=	22.20mm	=	2.22cm
1 inch	=	25.40mm	=	2.54cm
⅛ yard	=	11.43cm	=	0.11m
¼ yard	=	22.86cm	=	0.23m
⅜ yard	=	34.29cm	=	0.34m
½ yard	=	45.72cm	=	0.46m
⅝ yard	=	57.15cm	=	0.57m
¾ yard	=	68.58cm	=	0.69m
⅞ yard	=	80.00cm	=	0.80m
1 yard	=	91.44cm	=	0.91m

1⅛ yards	=	102.87cm	=	1.03m
1¼ yards	=	114.30cm	=	1.14m
1⅜ yards	=	125.73cm	=	1.26m
1½ yards	=	137.16cm	=	1.37m
1⅝ yards	=	148.59cm	=	1.49m
1¾ yards	=	160.02cm	=	1.60m
1⅞ yards	=	171.44cm	=	1.71m
2 yards	=	182.88cm	=	1.83m
2⅛ yards	=	194.31cm	=	1.94m
2¼ yards	=	205.74cm	=	2.06m
2⅜ yards	=	217.17cm	=	2.17m
2½ yards	=	228.60cm	=	2.29m
2⅝ yards	=	240.03cm	=	2.40m
2¾ yards	=	251.46cm	=	2.51m
2⅞ yards	=	262.88cm	=	2.63m
3 yards	=	274.32cm	=	2.74m
3⅛ yards	=	285.75cm	=	2.86m
3¼ yards	=	297.18cm	=	2.97m
3⅜ yards	=	308.61cm	=	3.09m
3½ yards	=	320.04cm	=	3.20m
3⅝ yards	=	331.47cm	=	3.31m
3¾ yards	=	342.90cm	=	3.43m
3⅞ yards	=	354.32cm	=	3.54m
4 yards	=	365.76cm	=	3.66m
4⅛ yards	=	377.19cm	=	3.77m
4¼ yards	=	388.62cm	=	3.89m
4⅜ yards	=	400.05cm	=	4.00m
4½ yards	=	411.48cm	=	4.11m
4⅝ yards	=	422.91cm	=	4.23m
4¾ yards	=	434.34cm	=	4.34m
4⅞ yards	=	445.76cm	=	4.46m
5 yards	=	457.20cm	=	4.57m

HOUSE of WHITE BIRCHES
PUBLISHERS SINCE 1947

Love to Dress Up 18" Doll Clothes is published by DRG, 306 East Parr Road, Berne, IN 46711. Printed in USA. Copyright © 2009 DRG. All rights reserved. This publication may not be reproduced in part or in whole without written permission from the publisher.

RETAIL STORES: If you would like to carry this pattern book or any other DRG publications, visit DRGwholesale.com

Every effort has been made to ensure that the instructions in this publication are complete and accurate. We cannot, however, take responsibility for human error, typographical mistakes or variations in individual work. Please visit ClotildeCustomerCare.com to check for pattern updates.

STAFF

Editor: Dianne Schmidt
Technical Editors: Angie Buckles, Marla Laux
Technical Artist: Connie Rand
Copy Supervisor: Michelle Beck
Copy Editors: Amanda Ladig, Mary O'Donnell
Graphic Arts Supervisor: Ronda Bechinski

Graphic Artists: Glenda Chamberlain, Edith Teegarden
Art Director: Brad Snow
Assistant Art Director: Nick Pierce
Photography Supervisor: Tammy Christian
Photography: Matthew Owen
Photo Stylist: Tammy Steiner

ISBN: 978-1-59217-282-5

456789